THE HOMELESSNESS OF A CHILD

for Annie

Ian

Other Books by Ian Gouge

Novels and Novellas

A Pattern of Sorts - Coverstory books, 2020
The Opposite of Remembering - Coverstory books, 2020
At Maunston Quay - Coverstory books, 2019
An Infinity of Mirrors - Coverstory books, 2018 (2nd ed.)
The Big Frog Theory - Coverstory books, 2018 (2nd ed.)
Losing Moby Dick and Other Stories - Coverstory books, 2017

Short Stories

Degrees of Separation - Coverstory books, 2018
Secrets & Wisdom - Paperback, 2017

Poetry

The Myths of Native Trees - Coverstory books, 2020
First-time Visions of Earth from Space - Coverstory books, 2019
After the Rehearsals - Coverstory books, 2018
Punctuations from History - Coverstory books, 2018
Human Archaeology - Paperback, 2017
Collected Poems (1979-2016) - KDP, 2017

Anthologies

New Contexts: 1 - Coverstory books, 2021
Triple Measures - Ian Gouge, K.M.Miller, Tom Furniss, Coverstory books, 2020
Oak Tree Alchemy - Coverstory books, 2019
Play for Three Hands - Tom Furniss, Ian Gouge, K.M.Miller, pamphlet 1981

IAN GOUGE

THE HOMELESSNESS OF A CHILD

Coverstory books

First published in paperback format by
Coverstory books, 2021

ISBN 978-1-8382321-1-5

Copyright © Ian Gouge 2021

The cover image is based on an original
photograph taken by the author © Ian Gouge
2021.

www.iangouge.com

www.coverstorybooks.com

Contents

III

❁

Foreword

By the time Ian Gouge went to university he had already lived in seventeen different places - houses, pre-fabs, flats, rooms of one sort or another - and all within the environs of the same two towns: Portsmouth and Gosport, on the south coast of England. No single location more than four miles from the next, between some you could have measured the distance in hundreds of yards. If you put a pin in a map for each, the resulting image would look like the aftermath of a rather well-played game of 'pin-the-tail-on-the-donkey' (see page 9).

A number of these accommodations had been emergency refuges provided by the Local Authority to stave off homelessness; two the 60s/70s equivalents of 'sofa surfing'. But in reality, every single residence proved temporary. Exactly at a time when a child needed security, the very notions of 'home', 'family' - even 'love' - were being challenged, their meanings redefined, shaken to their core; experiences which scarred both an upbringing and the future which followed it.

In the major thread of "The Homelessness of a Child", the poet reflects on that childhood, explores its events and repercussions. Inevitably it is both a passionate and dispassionate retelling, the latter a result of the detachment a young boy would learn to adopt in order to protect himself from the chaos of the world he was forced to inhabit.

I

Street Names We Navigated By

...was the word
and the word was
money
slithering and whispering forked-tongued
through the undergrowth of our lives

and when it spoke
slyly sibilant
they listened   entranced
bewitched by dreams that tomorrow would be different

later   and inevitably
we embarked on a cycle of wandering
               and settling
black-and-white episodes
continuously repeated
     on non-prime channels with poor reception
trailers delivered by a voice in their heads
     its silky seduction

this time

     next time

          tomorrow

          ❂

     Sackville   Gurnard   Cleveland

those first names etched in legend
as a boy might recite
the '66 cup-winning team

        Banks
    Cohen   Wilson
  Stiles   Charlton   Moore

after that
and the signal ferry crossing[1]
flat-bottomed   choppy
the pontoon nodding in approval
at our banishment
the sequence is blurred
street names running together
the random outcome of an unnamed game
with everything left to chance

Sackville
Gurnard   Cleveland
Cambridge   Anglesey   Seymour

Seaward   Parham
Prince of Wales   Avenue   Naish

St Vincent
Albert
Hamlet

each one begs a story
a fractured compendium of memory
hidden behind the privacy of brick walls
and masked in silent anguish

---

[1] Across the harbour, between Portsmouth and Gosport

Map of Portsmouth and Gosport, on the South Coast of England.

The fourteen locations referred to in "Street Names We Navigated By" and "Snapshots" are illustrated by small black flags. Those in Gosport covered a period of approximately twelve years (i.e. living an average of around 13 months in each).

Three other very temporary locations during that same 12-year period (council-funded hotels / hostels / B&Bs) are not shown. If they were, they would appear just outside of this map to the north-west.

In terms of scale, the distance between the outlying flags west-to-east is 8.2 km (approx.), and north-to-south 6.2 km (approx.). This means fourteen 'homes' in twenty years across an area of just 50 square km, the two in closest proximity to each other were just 400m apart.

Snapshots *(ages are always approximate)*

Sackville *(aged 0-4)*

ghostly memories
a small pavement-fronted house
a shield from the world

smiling blazered-boy
a pristine red pedal-car
steered all the way home

sandwiches were treats
dripping   sugar   red ketchup
strawberry jam / cheese

Gurnard *(aged 4-6)*

one year   soon to burn
ex-railway-uniformed Guy
guarding the hallway

in the back garden
scrub   a dented copper tub
bathing luxury

the '63 snow
its veneer coating the world
the dog belly-wet

at the blue lido
a leopard-skinned never-tanned
fish out of water

entranced by language
he explored discoveries
"what's for fucking tea?"

Christmas with measles
carried to the tinselled tree
no presents unwrapped

police combing hills
unaware   not being lost
but being searched for

Cleveland (aged 6-10)

fishing off the pier
mirage of the huge fish lost
to a plastic reel

last threepenny-bits
slipped into fun-fair machines
until they were gone

someone gave him boots
white when football shunned fashion
still he couldn't play

an eight-by-four board
became the world   train-tracks laid
inexhaustibly

later   the long walk
the Aladin's Cave pawn shop
his trains swapped for food

~ see *Chasing Grace, Elm Grove Library, The Art
of Skiving* & *Cinders*

Cambridge (aged 10)

toys wrapped in jumpers
a whole life's possessions in
a single suitcase

one compensation
shipwrecked at the Captain's   was
crossing in the bridge[2]

hand up   trying French
mangling half-understood words
causing derision

Anglesey (aged 10)

setting the standard
a house far too good for us
then always yearned for

chained to school lunches
the liver Miss made me eat
freedom's quid pro quo

~ see *Another Christmas* & *Alverstoke*

Seymour (aged 10-11)

matt green bus to Lee[3]
comfort in rough gear changes
predictably made

---

[2] the ferry between Gosport and Portsmouth

[3] Lee-on-the-Solent

by the army camp
the turn toward the bleak front
the ever-grey sea

it was desolate
a run-down no-man's-land of
faded seaside cheer

～ see *In Stanley Park, Passing Notes* & *Victory*

Seaward (aged 11-12)

in the creaking lift
to a flat where model planes
hung in the bedroom

so mesmerising
the harbour nine floors below
watching yachts   ferries

warships dressed in grey
funereal submarines
naval chess pieces

～ see *For Liz* & *Giro-scopic*

Parham (aged 12)

～ see *Stan, Stan, the Crackpot Man*

Prince of Wales (aged 12)

alone with echoes
of his impromptu concerts
singing Edelweiss

family now ghosts
except for war-scarred Arthur
Glad   her anchor George

china mantle dogs
in the parlour no-one used
but to cry at wakes

～ see *Gladys*

Avenue (aged 12-13)

through the flimsy door
upstairs to the three-roomed flat
and the thin z-bed

unfolded each night
creaking narrow host for sleep
fitful and fitting

～ see *Cross-country* & *Fifty-one Pounds*

Naish (aged 13-16)

squat at the lane's end
life trapped in drab grey panels
prefabricated

then weekend cycling
to test out a first freedom
football   chess   cricket

St Vincent (aged 16-18)

restless   cast adrift
lost in misunderstandings
and career false starts

a sign   the moped
with only one working break
top speed twenty-eight

memory holds fast
only to external things
the episodic

Albert (aged 18-21)

waiting for the bus
and a girl to break the seal
on a fledgling life

that she never came
proved the past imperious
moats unbridgeable

even poetry
failed to breach old defences
sunk pile-driven deep

Hamlet (aged 21)

building collages
scraps of paper fantasies
mirrored fractured life

on the bedroom wall
the painted Underground map
a form of escape

to never go back
acting out the final scene
Hamlet exit left

~ see *The Binding of the Sea*

Chasing Grace

enshrined in plastic blisters and gaudy cardboard
poorly moulded beads
Made in China
a cheap Post Office special

all unseen by a seven-year-old
sold on an idea
fabricating a birthday as an excuse
to buy the girl he loved a token
more of a statement than playground kiss-chase

jail-breaking school at lunchtime
running all the way home for his pennies
a romantic hero straight out of Hollywood
thinking he was Steve McQueen
seeking freedom on his Harley

in the same way McQueen still rides
his not escaping replayed year on year
he pursues re-imaginings of Grace
longing to be that boy again
but one wise enough to find her a better present

E lm Grove Library [4]

it sat back from the road   apologetically
barricaded by modest gardens and a low wall
a municipal bungalow
          the antithesis of splendour and promise

yet inside was a treasure trove
the spot the 'X' marked
yards of books on low-slung shelves
        child-high   alluring

feigning illness to bunk-off school again
the boy took possession
imagining a moat around 'A' to 'D'
then drawbridge up
honed-in on Blyton
          famous
              secret

what seeds were sown then
not those of adventure
but saplings of a different kind
      of imagination
          of invention
of the power of putting one word in front of another
and seeing where they took you

<hr>

[4] The site of the library has long since been redeveloped into University student accommodation.

The Art of Skiving School

playing his cards right
he'd feign illness Sunday tea-time
early enough to sow the seed
Monday morning's capitulation
born from a mother's concern

low-key the first day
a reprise performance in the evening
usually enough to secure Tuesday
if he made it to Wednesday
the whole week was in the bag

liberated
he spent time in made-up worlds
playing games
racing cars and horses
making models
invading the library

he was lucky
bright enough to get away with it

in days when eighty-percent attendance
went unpunished
school terms became fragmented   indistinct
stressful in the repeated angst of yet another first day back

even now he wonders what he might have become
had he knuckled down
                              and just tried

C linker

when we had money
we would bank-up the fire overnight
shielding priceless coal
with a blanket of cinders
saved from previous days

when we were lucky
the fire would still be glowing
in the morning
coaxed back to life
with a few scraps of wood

when unlucky
at least the room would be tepid
even if the ritual
of saving spent embers
needed to be reinitiated

watching money go up in smoke
as it turned to ash
was both temporary respite
against the cold
and a foretelling of the future

A nother Christmas

Then
Christmas arrived as an apology,
wrestled from tinsel-filled dreams
with obvious sleight-of-hand.
A prematurely balding tree embraced
the blooming of impossible colours
fairy lights' celebration
transmitted via morse-code flicker.

Yes
the typewriter's carriage return sang with its magical 'ding'
(just like the last machine you'd been forced to hock
harvesting cash for sliced white
and Cadbury's 'Smash'),
but the four-lane Scalextric
would have been more exciting
had you three friends to play it with.

Now
a lifetime beyond the giddiness of unwrapping,
past the inevitable repetition of
just what I wanted,
you see that passion play for what it was,
an abundance of 'sorry',
scant compensation for another year
of turmoil and heartbreak.

A lverstoke

elevated above the road
even the church excluded us
>not that we were interested
>foreign to upbringings
>invested in such promises

walking round the lanes
peering through windows of shops never entered
feeling like outcasts or refugees
shipwrecked on a foreign coast
abandoned
>as much without hope as without money
>or the right shoes

unbeknownst
it formed a template
like a model village in which impossible people lived
something to aspire too
a tattoo to be magicked into reality
>or a scab to be picked at

as if a commentary on his time there
after he left they condemned the school
>its fabric unsafe
turning the land to more profitable use
and dreams to rubble

In Stanley Park

at one point
a circular embrace of rhododendrons aspiring to be trees
branches conjoined into a single crown
and at their heart
a hollowed space
a secret den

inside
boughs grow   horizontally
or have been cajoled there
persuaded into love seats

Lynda sits
fiery blonde hair threatening orange
brown well-deep eyes
the lips he longs to kiss

eight feet is a chasm in this shady calm
the dried earth between them
                                    quicksand
forbidding any move
        to hold her face in his hands

but that is the man talking
the man who now knows time is precious
        and life passes as quickly as the voices
        that drifted in from the path nearby
who knows what it's like
        to hold someone close
        to feel the beating of their heart

it seems unfair
such wisdom was denied an eleven-year-old boy
who needed it then
so much more than the man does now

years later
he saw her in a supermarket car park
she was older
yet her hair still that burnished colour
and he dared to wonder
how life would have been lived
if a young boy had stood
and walked eight feet

Passing Notes

by the time it was confiscated
      part-way through an irrelevant historical event
      from the nineteenth century
the sheet was already brittle
as if all the unfolding
              signing
                 re-folding
had aged it   robbed it of integrity
its feint blue-veined lines
      corrupted by harsh ballpoints
      and manufactured anger

forgoing the Georgians
in the tense silence
Mr Patterson unfolded it one more time
      weighed the assertion
          light as paper   heavy as lead
      glanced at him   waiting

giving nothing away
not even the thinnest of smiles
he placed it in his jacket pocket
      a submission for break-time staffroom chit-chat
      a joke with Miss Taylor-Smith

it was only later he discovered its contents
a rebuke for ditching his girlfriend
nearly all the other girls had endorsed

Vivienne had not
and the following week
they went to explore HMS Victory together
      a twelve-year-old's statement of defiance
              and his classmates' vindication

Victory

off the ferry and through the dock gates
the ship all black-and-yellow precision
half its one-hundred canon pointing
across the harbour to where he lived

almost perpendicular
the stairs forced you down backwards
navigating by trust into increasing darkness
ceiling beams ever-lower
cots too small even at twelve
and in the sick bay
the floor painted red
to make blood look like water

bizarrely it was a place to take girls
forced to hold hands as you ducked
and squeezed into small spaces
shoulders touching in the polite crush

yet even in that respect
'Victory' proved something of a misnomer
the stairs
            the darkness
                        the cramped discomfort
                                    the painted floor
less a triumph
                        and more a metaphor for life

For Liz

fifty years since

years smuggled illegally across the border
disguising themselves
            with incident   accident   crisis
and from nowhere I am reminded of
an effervescent girl
who laughed as if she were party to secrets
            kept from the rest of us
who courted scandal with short skirts
            being the first to wear a bra
who took me to the park that sunny Saturday
            and introduced me to my first wet kiss

I have felt guilty all these years
for the way I cast you aside
a twelve-year-old's fear victorious over everything

how wistful is this
recognising at the other end of time
how much of life you owned
            and how much of it you offered me

G iro-scopic

once
when the Thursday Giro failed to arrive
not having the bus fare
they walked the four miles
to seek salvation in the drab social security office
taking a number
      sitting on harsh plastic chairs
          waiting their turn

      to beg

then unrewarded
to walk all the way back
those same four miles in reverse
her purse
      empty as promises

what did they talk about
all that way
        there and back

S tan, Stan, the Crackpot Man [5]

when they walked into the parlour he spat on the floor
as if it were common-place   as traditional
as the fug from cabbage stewing in the kitchen

his eyes   like his legs   were misaligned
and when he shuffled toward you
you could never be sure where he was looking

or how

his accent   East European
as heavy as the aroma seeping from the walls
unfathomable to a child who still needed to believe in something

at the end of the street the timber yard
was the boy's favourite place for a while
somewhere he could revel in the majesty
of the planed and square cut
and cleanse his lungs with the heavenly smell of wood

they were not in Parham Road long
and later heard the story of how Stan
          perhaps finally realising how adrift he had become
raided his own electricity meter with a crowbar
evading police by clambering over garden fences
neither legs nor eyes
          any hindrance to his brief bid for freedom

---

[5] The title of a poem I wrote later, and subsequently read out in an English lesson. I
was twelve years old.

G ladys

You could have built walls from her cakes,
carved them into precisely defined slabs;
they were large, chocolatey and oddly grey
with the pitted consistency of breeze block.
Cutting the first slice after tea was a ritual,
a special treat for post-school Mondays.

In a house of twisted personalities
exaggerated by the mental shrapnel of war,
her laugh was resistant to misery and disease,
a cackle that challenged you to defy it,
exploding to deafen the under-breath chunter
of a brother who'd lost more than weight in Burma.

I felt for Uncle George, marooned like me,
as long-suffering as he was grey-topped tall,
handcuffed to a recurrent Poe-like nightmare
from which he could never escape -
or from which she would never release him.
I was too young then to decipher life.

One by one, death smuggled them away,
though only after I had been partially rescued.
Arthur's going finally ended his bitter war,
and not even her laugh could save George,
silently eaten away from the inside
all the while defending his back-bent dignity.

Suffering, punishment and freedom
I discovered later; a three-card-trick
played chest-close, ace hidden up the sleeve.
In a theatre beyond all vanquishing,
she rescued a child who loved her cakes
and who later missed the chance to thank her.

Cross-country

in the beginning it was a dodge
to avoid the threat of rugby's crunch
the humiliation of a limp tackle

they ran across football pitches and out the back gate
beyond the copse into the buffeting arms of the shore road

the going was easy and flat until they peeled onto the beach
crunching beneath the old pier   struggling on the stones
the feet-sucking shingle mocking their pace

finding the path again felt like salvation
though the old fort still a mile away
and only there the turn for home

somewhere up ahead   Negus unbeatable
rumoured to have won the race to lose his virginity too
crossed into another country
his one-off partner just the girl to dispense such charity

struggling back through the gate
would often coincide with rugby's conclusion
though if they were lucky they would get to the showers first
Negus already dressed and gone
                              beating them to that too

Fifty-one Pounds

the exchange
>coin for a flimsy carbon-copied
>toilet-roll-sized sheet
>covered in times of assignations
>and Bond-like call-signs

then
one weekend
Newbury
>New Member
>Roman Holiday
>one to beat Pendil in the fourth

fifty-five pence magicked into fifty-one pounds
notes spread on the kitchen table
laughter freed by lucre

it was the culmination of years of practice
Saturday mornings working at the paper
thinking you were studying form
afternoons in front of World of Sport
a white-quiffed Dickie Davies
the glue between football   the ITV 7   and the wrestling

winning
was all guesswork really
the vagaries of luck
>good and bad
all the while
paying the piper of addiction-soaked DNA

The Binding of the Sea

would the tide never stop coming in
inching ever higher as the months passed

there were only two roads out
each burdened with over-familiarity
all novelty quagmire-sunk as if
       the peninsula had capitulated
       and the sea invaded the land

going further afield
they sought pubs in out-of-the-way locations
explorers for the source of something
until the travelling became all there was

as he broke away
the sound of waves followed him
       university in a port town
       volunteering in a sub-Saharan Atlantic village
       his first real job in a cathedral city near the coast

       a West Indian island perhaps the ultimate capitulation

later
the irony of ending up in the middle
land everywhere and the coast out of reach
       exposing his longing for the chill breeze
       the sounds of feet on shingle
       the salted aroma of the sea

II

The Skip

rusting through paint-broken gaps
it juts into the road
hazardous on a blind bend
the only warning
      a badly-located orange cone
      its colour diluted by too much sun

the letters at its rim are flaked
inadequate clues
divulging nothing of purpose or ownership

curious
you look inside
      semi-guilty
afraid to be accused of scavenging for unworn-out things

in the abject and disorganised discard
      the odd flash of colour
          no more than heyday hints
there   a crushed box from a childhood toy
      the semi-hidden tangle of unattached wires
      the frame of something you cannot place
      the outline of a book
all are compromised
      like a puzzle with half the pieces thrown away

prompted
you remember the detritus in your pockets
      a used train ticket
      an old shopping list
      a pen dry of ink
you toss them furtive to the skip
where their landing makes no sound
      an accumulation instantly invisible

tomorrow
you will return
   to find the skip still there
   to add to the collection
the paint flaked a little more
   the hazard undiminished
     the story indecipherable

Sidings

they arc from sight with bizarre elegance
an overgrown divergence
designated to home the unwanted
                              or the forgotten

weeds climb rusting axles
clogging memories of motion
and birds flit in the eerie silence
to reserve a first-class nesting site

Black Coffee on the 7:49

the bequest of storms
named as if an old friend
            or the grouchy next-door-neighbour
flooded fields pass silently
waiting to be appreciated
sketched by latter-day Constables
            Swans on the Trent
though what you take for a river
                              was once a road

microwaved hot
coffee from the other side of the world
flown-in to fill my non-recyclable cup

I let it cool
as I watch the world slip away outside

Brown-to-green[6]

embracing a road swathe-cut through the landscape
trees whisper their colour to the world

> *look at us*
> *we are changing*

by unspoken pact
they transform themselves
into an act of remembrance
recalling other years
the always shorter journeys into summer
                              blink and you've missed it

we never make enough of March I said
too busy talking to see it disappear
even knowing the moment would soon come
for the annual echo
where did that go?

why should this year's turning be any different

and yet
            there is promise in this verdancy

driving through a tunnel of March trees
on a road swathe-cut through the landscape
I listen to the blessing of colour

---

[6] Written - ironically - one week before the first national Covid-19 lockdown in March 2020

3 a.m. fog

beyond the glass
sodium filters through the fog like pin-pricks of promise
there is comfort in knowing
streets will emerge
lights will go out
       another dawn
              another chance

I wake again at three
and rouse myself
heeding advice to be occupied
that writing something down is a salve

the fog seeps through the windows
and swamps me as I sit
drinking decaf tea
listening to the click of the keyboard
seeking my own illuminations
waiting for the sun to rise

The only reason

I wonder when certainty abandoned her

      as she walked towards the tube
            still cocooned by our brief farewell kiss

      or later   pulling pyjamas from a drawer
          in her studio flat

      or after days   or weeks   or years
          chiding herself for her foolishness

pyjamas would have suited her modesty
soft winceyette   pastel-coloured   subtly-patterned

she would have unbuttoned them slowly
as if each button were a step into the unknown
      a risk   a wager
and then taking my hand   trembling   into her own
placed it on a breast
      laying bare the truth kept hidden all those months
      just as she had whispered it when she left

      the only reason I'm not crying
      is because I know I'll see you again

Clowne, Derbyshire

there should be big shoes to fill
cheeks rouged
lips alarmingly red

instead   a Tesco
hunkered down off a side-street
ashamed to have landed there by mistake

I run along a road that goes nowhere
past pavement-kissing terraces
a shabby field touting cheap horse shit

and pause by misaligned lights at the tricky junction
eyes chasing the number-plates of cars
to fix them in ancient history   pre-Tesco

then I turn to retrace my steps
running faster away than I had arrived

Deconstruction

we breach the outer shell
with theories designed to fracture and fragment
to expose the masquerade

the new legend says
there is treasure within

unfulfilled
we scan the broken husk
and all for what

to reveal a wizened kernel
       the antithesis of beauty

we would reconstruct it if we could
reconstitute sense and sensibility
weigh an unblemished second chance
to shut out the empty whisperings
and the pretence of where meaning surely lies

Fathom

an unseen voice calls the measure
from somewhere in the fog

six   *six*   *five*

numbers become heavily laden words
a substance about them
as they slip from six to five

he understands the consequence
if the shout is *two*

still
he stands and listens
as if no movement makes a difference

and from nowhere
he suddenly wishes there had been boatswain
who might have prevented
his running aground with Barbara

five   *six*   *six*

shapes move in the fret
no more than ghostly blurs

were they to blow hard
would the fog clear
might they alter course and steer for home
might Barbara yet be there
ready to forgive him

how is it possible to fathom such things

five   *four*   *three*

Mascara vs. Tattoos

I am going to be this person for a while
applicator thickened with the stuff of dreams
transforms my eyes to become someone else

look at me   at not-me
me as rock star   as hot dude / chick
challenging   exciting

be seduced by this other side
Pandora unlocked
someone else for us to play with

I am going to be this person for always
permanently etched
with a tableau of images

resolute ink veneer
soaked to the skin
my grain invisible

love   hate   a Celtic knot
if now I can't remember why
how can this still be me?

Failures of Crimping

at the edges
attempts at precision
indentations aspiring to perfection
our ambition blind-baked
against the inevitable corruption of heat

watching the clock count down
recall the flour-dusting of language
how we cajoled   pressed one word against another
striving for a pact
to seal in the contents

hopeful and oven-gloved
we rescue our creation from the furnace
marvel at its golden crust
remain dismayed at the crumbling
meaning calcified on the oven's floor

The Seven of Hearts

the cellophane crackles
      refuses to yield even after it has been breached
         then splits when you least expect it

they fall to the table haphazardly
and you sift semi-expertly looking for jokers
      flamboyant   untrustworthy

kings and queens slide reassuringly in your hands
perfectly aloof   tanned
like reality game-show contestants
    minor celebrities
    who'd do anything for the big prize
jacks seem to wink
      not knaves without reason

as ever
you never know how many shuffles are enough

flirtingly passive as you juggle them
    they become stiffly resistant to your hesitant faro

is that how it's going to be then
    unpredictable   moody   fickle

you have decided to use them for one game
then return them virtually unsullied to their box
accompanied by the scoresheet
        their history
    your gloss in the margin

perhaps it had been a famous victory
when later you recall how the game had hinged
on the draw of the seven of hearts

Variations

(i)

Elgar plays "The Enigma" on spoons rescued from Geller
hammered straight by an amateur blacksmith
with a passion for buxom sopranos

if the notes are a little wayward
you forgive them given you can eat trifle
with the instruments of their making

I'd like to see you do that with a cello
someone says stifling a laugh
and you wonder if they've been at the sherry

if it were an audition Elgar would have failed
no credit given for composition or commitment
nor the imaginative use of second-hand cutlery

(ii)

a hangover shaped the clock-face that way
sliding off the table   a metaphor for a mind
        struggling to keep a hold on things

he twirls unevenly curled moustaches
consolation in knowing reputation
        demotes incompetence before intent

yet there's something alluring about
bold unsophisticated colours   their sharp contrast
        both a promise and a threat

and from somewhere a melody he can't quite place
as if a string is untuned   or someone
        has bent a hammer in a baby grand

(iii)

he had begged a smile but had to settle for less
his best jokes betraying him
                and even arriving at one sitting cross-gartered
                        failed to generate a spark

knowing the end-product would be inadequate
he resorted to amusing himself
                by bending tricks of draughtsmanship
                        into enigmatic sleight-of-hand

it was all frustratingly amateurish of course
sacrificing time for the merely commercial
                a portrait of the ungrateful wife
                        of a semi-important merchant

(iv)

his ally
hammered home the message
about stripping back
his unforgiving pencil attacking words
                its marks locusts in a feeding frenzy

a shallow drawer
became hospice for the vanquished
remembrance of what had been lost
less for his own benefit
                than posterity's sanity

England his elopement
proved no wasteland at all
his dowry a gifting of place into legend
like variations whose first notes everybody knows
                no matter how badly they are played

(v)

if his own family had betrayed him like that
he would have taken a different line
an abdication less likely to backfire

still
it was cathartic to work things through
according to another's interpretation

profitable too

the irony hadn't escaped him
falling into fortune by mistake
a seed fertilised in an idle moment
                more luck than calling

never short of material
his rhythms mimic'd the people he knew
recycling old stories with a new twist
grateful his children had never bequeathed him a plot-line

except once

the ghost that haunted him

Shall We Dance

woken this morning by two pigeons
tap-dancing on the dormer ridge tiles
Astaire and Rogers honing a routine

pirouetting
she was lighter on her feet
weaving slender wing-arcs through the air
with an imaginary boa
while he
        feathers on the tuxedo-side of grey
circled clumsily cooing *look at me*
as if discovering something for the first time

just like a man

beneath millions of roofs
dances of indeterminate duration
played out against the backdrop of office or kitchen
        garden or shed
        lounge or library
            or bedroom
screenplays varying only in context
nuanced for circumstance
or clumsily rehashed like repeats
on a bargain-basement channel
episodes that blend into one
where the ending is given away in the opening credits

tentatively I begin my own dance once again
striving for invention and finesse
my shoes black-polished to within an inch of their lives
my dress-shirt white beyond white
my bow impeccably tied
and as I weave and circle feigning competence
my partner   who is all words   laughs

striving for an American Smooth or Argentine Tango
all I manage is a ham-fisted Conga
stumbling across the page
      tripping on the metre
            misplacing a comma

The River Eden, Appleby-in-Westmoreland, 2020[7]

the smell of new-mown grass is a blade-sharp promise
made without condition
drifting across the sparkling river
whose flooding is both memory and threat

clinging to the wreckage of a crisis
our desperation seeks benefits
as if justification's the thing
      less of this
            or more of that

whatever

in the smell of new-mown grass is a promise
tomorrow
      waiting to be made again

---

[7] written in the Summer between the first two waves of the Covid-19 pandemic

Identity Parade

you come to me in a dream
and in your face
the features of all those
I have ever loved
and in the curve of your hips
my greedy fingers seek contours
like searching for braille
on a map without a legend

waking offers no rescue
from the whisperings of the past
and I replay your many names
associate disappointments
with snapshots made from fading negatives
worn through in a well-thumbed album
suffer the haunting of promises made
and left unrequited

Waiting for Sunrise

through the attic Velux
a pre-dawn silhouette punctured by marquisette
the contours of the landscape blurred
in a monotone wash of Payne's Grey

the clock
ticks
like the taunting of a playground bully
knowing they are beyond the law

or are the law

I wait for the sunrise
and for something to arrive   or go away

often things are easier
in pre-dawn silhouettes punctured by marquisette

All Things Considered

And still the clock ticks
its resilient march sounding out across the room
swaddling your recumbent body
       oblivious   unconscious.

Tick.   Tick.   Tick.

Is there
locked away in the vault
      for which only you have the key
the replaying of scenes,
a highlight reel perhaps
all J Arthur Rank or Powell and Pressburger:
      the Blitz
      your first wedding
      giving birth.

Is it only trauma you remember
or are there highlights too
picked out in gaudy technicolour?

If so, I struggle to imagine them.

You played against a world
expert in dealing marked cards
      from the bottom of the deck
your meagre opportunities trumped at every turn.

Trick.   Trick.   Trick.

Perhaps this is your finally victory,
unacknowledged sores and bed-wetting
a small price to pay for pale oblivion.

After-words

then your words came tumbling out
like a river in full spate
a waterfall driving down into a pool
carved deep by the force of their syllables
and though you sat at its edge
playing the part of a detached observer
admiring the landscape   the picturesqueness of it all
there was no escaping the spray
rising like a mist
as if the words had broken on impact
and re-formed into something else
undeniable   unavoidable
and when you stood to go
unsure if you were glad to be leaving or not
you found that you were drenched
the remnants of words
permeating beneath the surface of your skin

Quieted

one day it will be too late
and all those things I should have said
or wanted to say
will be lost
because I will not be here to say them
nor remember they needed to be said
in the first place

Encore (or, I may have passed you on the streets of York)

for John Birtwhistle

I do not know you now,
half a lifetime between the people we once were;
a fragile connection even then
surely shaken loose by time.

Memory striving to keep afloat
- the ship holed beneath the waterline -
names are the splintered decking to which we cling
breathing between the rhythm of the waves
that threaten to engulf us.

Is it acceptable
- feelings anaesthetised by all the years -
to confess I didn't quite get you the way others did
(not that you probably gave a shit).
Yet it might be nice to meet again,
a new first-time
imbued with legacies
we've both earned and spent since then;
just two old guys coming together
invigorated by / drowned in
echoes of the fire and enthusiasm of youth.

R ecuperation

increasingly feint
the piper's tune seduces still
visions of the unattainable
we kid ourselves are yet within our grasp

each time a decibel dies
turn to a new leaf in a well-thumbed book
bereft but for a few loose sketches
        feint marks on feint lines

a splinter of you
wants to scream at the injustice
to find a new swear-word
knowing   like most things   'fuck' has lost its impact

bleeding still
you shift your position gingerly
as if protecting something precious
yet certain   in the end   doing so will make no difference

A fter Boxing Day

is that benevolence or pity
in the dulled eyes staring back
faceted with the scars of past events

yesterday passed
one to both enjoy and to endure
this morning's eyes headlining
that these days endurance is the key

playing out the pantomime
creases craze the fractals of his skin
and he cannot help but wonder
were those lines to conjoin and encircle him
become the barbed-wire about his life
what calamity might befall

is that benevolence or pity
in the dulled eyes that stare back
and buried in those furrows
a tracing of past events
unavoidable

The Promise of Alexandria

fooled by the green of imagined palms
and the whisper of a breeze
time mirages before me like an oasis I could almost touch

wiping sweat from my eyes
I recalibrate
and all I see is sand
folding and unfolding on itself
in perpetual motion

how am I supposed to make sense of that

the other day
Ice Cold in Alex on the television
a quartet trapped in a mesmeric desert
and the old ambulance   Katy
sliding back down a dune
the handbrake unapplied

I feel like Captain Anson
one more churn of the handle
inching the old girl back up
tantalised by the promise of the view from the top

III

The Cricket

In mis-matched mugs, tea
- too weak, too strong -
sits alongside crumb-dusted plates
cradling the remnants of tradition:
sandwiches, cake, the sausage rolls
for which they had all headed
the locusts of the Away-team.
Reputations are made in the pavilion
rather than on the field of play,
yorkers and cover-drives bowled over
by the untainted reputation
of Madge's Victoria Sponge.
They still speak in hushed tones
of the weekend it was made by someone else.

Dissecting the first innings
men in whites
take conversational guard from personal perspectives
volume and chattiness correlating to wickets and runs,
except for their ex-star pace-man who plays on past reputation
and is simply glad to be there
entitled to a ham salad
and a handful of crisps.

Second-sensing the clock
the openers rise and return their empties
to the hatch beyond which wives
- engaged in entirely different confrontations -
wash and wipe,
compare flamboyant notes on children's progress,
exaggerated plans for holidays.
The Number Three follows after a respectful pause
leaving the Next-Man-In the age-old dilemma
as to when he should pad-up:
too early shows lack of confidence,

too late, he might be caught out.
The opposition watch for him to move,
looking for clues as to their chances
of defending one-six-three for eight.
Then the cacophony of spikes on the pavilion steps,
the ritual of umpires donning coats and counting stones,
fielders' practice-catching - the mirage of professionalism -
before they all head out to the square
like a flotilla of small boats on a rescue mission.

To save what, the match?
To celebrate the sanctity of Madge's Victoria
and the efforts of all the ladies?
To provide an environment for kids
to play at being Daddy
and butcher that late cut for which he longs to be famous?

No.
Against dwindling interest
and the lure of the electronic
this is about the preservation of England,
and when the umpire calls "play"
they know they are safe for another week at least.

The Poet Laureate's Lament

Somewhere
an anonymous Committee made their irrefutable decision,
the Chairman then fumbling in a dusty drawer
for the plastic badge to pin on the lapel of the winner
- wasn't it a competition, after all?
Buffing it with the inside of a sleeve
the new Laureate tries to make it shine.
Lipstick on a pig.

Laureate: "an award for outstanding creative achievement",
"wreathed as a mark of honour",
"a member of the British royal household".

They have to take him seriously now.

He recalls boys who patrolled school corridors
their air of invincibility gifted
by the small bright red circle that boasted "PREFECT"
(and which he always misread as 'Perfect');
the uniform of a super-hero
investing powers beyond everyone's understanding.
Is that what this new trophy will do,
elevate his words to another level?

Instead he finds them asking him to pronounce
on things he has no interest in or doesn't understand,
taking his word as gospel,
tablets of poetry handed down from on high.
It's a cross someone has to bear.

So he trails through fêtes and garden parties
premières and festivals
wearing his pencil down to a stub,
churning out what is expected;
kudos for platitudes and tat.

And after a while
he longs to be rid of the badge,
but when his fingers search for the clasp
he finds it welded to his skin
true separation only possible in death.

So he determines to write a poem about dying
and demonstrate his mastery of free verse,
the piece for which he will be remembered
long after the next vote and
the Chairman's retrieval of a duplicate trophy.

If only he could find the time
with a supermarket to open in Bolton
tomorrow.

The New-Build

"Make thee an ark of gopher wood; rooms shalt thou make in the ark, and shalt pitch it within and without with pitch." - Genesis 6:14

If it's not one thing it's another
his wife's favourite maxim
designed to cover every eventuality.
At the small formica table she kneads dough,
bemoans their moving from the city,
ties herself up in the knots of her past life,
the life before him.
It never rained until I met you
a contestable complaint.

He wades through omnipresent mud
to a makeshift garden office
- a windowless Portakabin with limited ventilation -
and questions inadequate plans,
listens to the thrumming on the roof,
antics of cooped-up caravan-children,
the restlessness of animals
corralled outside.

This is not the future he was sold.

Rumour runs in rivulets;
whispers say it's the same everywhere,
banks bursting onto non-existent floodplains
where families like his sit and wait
uninsured against An Act of God.

Winter Fodder

Three birds on the feeder this morning
democratically equidistant
without the need for debate or
arbitration from a parliament of owls.

[Such a complex image for the modern era,
wisdom and the offices of government.]

When the robin arrives
the trio zig-zag back to their clans,
tell-tale flight patterns
a compendium of darts and deviations
bursts of tribal action
instinctive frantic fluttering
and habitual fear.

The robin
- chest puffed out
trying to look presidential
in its red-breasted tie -
perches, scans, sings *look at me*
deigns to eat
until established in his territory,
then disregards fake food -
circular fat balls a bribe for lesser species
those black-bench tits perhaps,
or democrats.

Overhead
a blue belies the crust on the pond,
a sky supremely indifferent
to the chattering classes
masters or slaves.

Either side of the Gutter

Framed by walls of utilitarian brick
they sit on plastic chairs outside the Working Men's Club
and smoke, bemoaning traffic clogging the arterial junction
diesels born from the privilege of a city regeneration programme.
Hacking unfiltered Capstan-coughs
they reminisce about the Old Days of sometime-jobs
and swap stories of bosses and foremen
every noun prefixed with their favourite adjective,
a word become second-nature and
particularly suitable in these dark days
of Eastern European 'invasion'.
And so they relished the chance to have their say,
basing their vote on a past that never existed,
and the fact that Nigel Whatsisname likes a pint.

Later
unsettled dust gives them cause
to complain about pensions and the price of fags,
narratives informed by Red Top editorials
scanned only when they make it beyond
the inflated assets of page three.

You could have been like that,
biased toward a father's genes,
more out of work than in,
addicted to cigarettes and traps two and six
in the first race at Hackney,
Saturday morning's High Church.
Instead, you sit waiting at the lights
outside the Working Men's Club,
air-conditioned in your Audi,
bemoaning from an alternative viewpoint
fucking Brexit.

The Judgement

"If I mistook my literary escapades
for legitimate adventures in the belly of the beast
do not misread them as premeditated follies
but rather the innocent output of the ham-fisted."

An honest confession or some linguistic sleight-of-hand designed to throw us off the scent, whining and wheedling, aiming to be gifted absolution or excuse unquenchable addiction?

Hidden away in some spine-broken notebook, exhibits we suspect he would prefer not held to the light; their irregular warp and weft and a certain looseness in the fabric, exposure he is keen to avoid.

In a rudimentary image crudely drawn, one such offering presents - in the middle of a pedestrian bridge - an iron gate padlock-shut, its key long since slipped through trouser-pocket holes, gutter-fallen and kicked unknowingly toward the oblivion of the drains. Soaked by rain and decomposing autumn leaves, it wallows in an overcoat of mud while he stands pretentiously examining the gate, cold ungloved hands rattling the frame, hoping for hinges to give way under the modesty of his onslaught. He envies the greenness on the gate's other side as if there were a better rainbow to which he could upgrade.

All superstitious nonsense.

Rain chafes as hard on that side as this, the wind's howling unmoderated; yet in its whistling he pretends to messages.

"If it is a crime to have tried to depict a fraction of things seen or felt
then I plead guilty, beg the sentence be not harsh,
and ask consideration be given in recognition of a good war waged."

Pathetic pleadings; as if they could educate the margins in a reputable court of law!

"So it is a trial then; guilty until proven innocent.
There are circumstances to be considered in my defence;
'contributing factors'."

Such as?

"As a child, teachers who would
resort to the slipper for extra-curricular learning;
times' tables written out on blackboards,
and spellings tested weekly!
Isn't that torture worthy of something?
And bread, hard on the second day, off by the third.
Now it lasts forever, hormone-injected,
protected in American-style freezers.
Or gears on buses that ground when they changed;
and spinning the handle on shoulder-slung machines,
conductors dispensing flimsy tickets.
There was always paper, and carbon copies;
library books with pasted labels, columns for stamps
thumped down as you left the building,
reading permission slips.
We played football in the unforgiving street;
spent all our pocket money in funfair slots;
chased girls hopelessly, never catching one
- especially later in our Saturday-night Travolta-failings.
We chanted on terraces and threw up
in the backs of friends' cars
after three-too-many pints;
we scrabbled for meaning in the fog of growing up
always assuming we had it grasped
before it slipped through our fingers.
Surely all that experience is worth something?"

The judge - a spitting image of the defendant - dons a black cape to
pass sentence; 'Life' the inevitable consequence.

Acknowledgements

Previous publications:

- "Variations" was first published in *New Contexts: 1*, Coverstory books, 2021
- "The Skip" was first published in *Geography is Irrelevant*, Stairwell Books 2020
- "Clinker" (as "Cinders") and "For Liz" (as "For Liz Darby") were first published in *The Myths of Native Trees*, by Ian Gouge, Coverstory books, 2020
- "Gladys" was first published in *First-time Visions of Earth from Space*, by Ian Gouge, Coverstory books, 2019

Lightning Source UK Ltd.
Milton Keynes UK
UKHW011419060122
396705UK00001B/62

9 781838 232115